A BASIC BOOK OF
AMPHIBIANS
LOOK-AND-LEARN

by
W.P. MARA

LIST OF PHOTOGRAPHERS

The following is a list of the photographers whose work appears in this book:
William B. Allen, Jr., R. D. Bartlett, Thad Beaumont, James P. Bogart, Dr.
Warren E. Burgess, Jon W. Church, John Coborn, Sorin Damian, George Dibley,
Guido Dingerkus, E. Elkan, Paul Freed, Michael Gilroy, David Green, Ken
Lucas, W. P. Mara, Jim Merli, Dr. Sherman A. Minton, Jr., W. Mudrack, Kenneth
T. Nemuras, Ivan Sazima, P. W. Scott, R. S. Simmons, Mark Smith, Robert
Sprackland, Karl H. Switak, J. Visser, L. Wischnath, and Robert T. Zappalorti.
The artwork on page 12 was done by John R. Quinn.

Cover photograph of *Epipedobates silverstonei* by A. van den Nieuwenhuizen.

Distributed in the UNITED STATES to the Pet Trade by T.F.H. Publications, Inc., One T.F.H.
Plaza, Neptune City, NJ 07753; distributed in the UNITED STATES to the Bookstore and
Library Trade by National Book Network, Inc. 4720 Boston Way, Lanham MD 20706; in
CANADA to the Pet Trade by H & L Pet Supplies Inc., 27 Kingston Crescent, Kitchener,
Ontario N2B 2T6; Rolf C. Hagen Ltd., 3225 Sartelon Street, Montreal 382 Quebec; in
CANADA to the Book Trade by Macmillan of Canada (A Division of Canada Publishing
Corporation), 164 Commander Boulevard, Agincourt, Ontario M1S 3C7; in the United
Kingdom by T.F.H. Publications, PO Box 15, Waterlooville PO7 6BQ; in AUSTRALIA AND
THE SOUTH PACIFIC by T.F.H. (Australia), Pty. Ltd., Box 149, Brookvale 2100 N.S.W.,
Australia; in NEW ZEALAND by Brooklands Aquarium Ltd. 5 McGiven Drive, New
Plymouth, RD1 New Zealand; in Japan by T.F.H. Publications, Japan—Jiro Tsuda, 10-12-
3 Ohjidai, Sakura, Chiba 285, Japan; in SOUTH AFRICA by Multipet Pty. Ltd., P.O. Box
35347, Northway, 4065, South Africa. Published by T.F.H. Publications, Inc.
Manufactured in the United States of America by T.F.H. Publications, Inc.

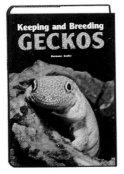

TS-166, 192 pgs, 175+ photos   KW-132, 96 pgs, 40+ photos   KW-002, 96 pgs, 70+ photos   TS-154, 192 pgs, 175+ photos

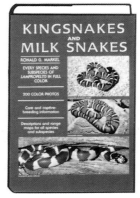

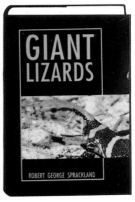

TS-128, 592 pgs, 1400+ photos   TS-125, 144 pgs, 200+ photos   TS-145, 288 pgs, 280+ photos

T-112, 64 pgs, 40+ photos   KW-127, 96 pgs, 80+ photos   PS-316, 128 pgs, 50+ photos   CO-041, 96 pgs, 80+ photos   TU-024, 64 pgs, 50+ photos

SK-017, 64 pgs, 40+ photos   YF-115, 36 pgs, 20+ photos   PS-311, 96 pgs, 45+ photos   SK-015, 64 pgs, 35+ photos

These and thousands of other animal books have been published by TFH. TFH is the world's largest publisher of animal books. You can find our titles at the same place you bought this one, or write to us for a free catalog.

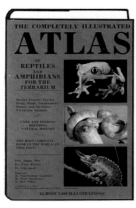

H-1102, 830 pgs, 1800+ photos   TS-165, VOL. I, 655 pgs, 1850+ photos   TS-165, VOL. II, 655 pgs, 1850+ photos

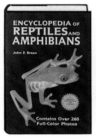

PS-207, 230 pgs, B&W illus.   H-935, 576 pgs, 260+ photos   PS-876, 384 pgs, 175+ photos   KW-197, 128 pgs, 110+ photos

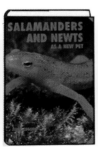

TW-115, 256 pgs, 180+ photos   CO-0438, 96 pgs, 80+ photos   TU-023, 64 pgs, 50+ photos   PB-126, 64 pgs, 32+ photos   AP-925, 160 pgs, 120+ photos

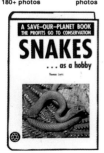

TT-001, 96 pgs, 80+ photos   J-007, 48 pgs, 25+ photos   TU-015, 64 pgs, 50+ photos   TW-111, 256 pgs, 180+ photos

These and thousands of other animal books have been published by TFH. TFH is the world's largest publisher of animal books. You can find our titles at the same place you bought this one, or write to us for a free catalog.

INTRODUCTION

The hobby of herpetology has evolved into one word, *herpetoculture*, which by definition means "the keeping and propagating of reptiles and amphibians in a domestic setting." In today's hobby there is a somewhat one-sided view of things—reptiles are much more popular than amphibians. Reliable statistics tell us snakes and lizards far outnumber frogs, toads, salamanders, and other amphibians in terms of what is being kept and bred. This is rather unfortunate. In this book you will be introduced to the wonderful world of amphibians and discover what fascinating creatures they are. Afterward, you may find yourself thinking about keeping a poison frog or a Spotted Salamander rather than a garter snake or a Leopard Gecko.

➤ Frogs and toads belong to the order Anura (thus they are often called "anurans") and are characterized by such traits as having strong hindlimbs designed for jumping, stout forelimbs and a short body, a very short vertebral column, and, in the males of most species, the possession of a vocal sac used to call for a female during the breeding season. Shown here are two Cope's Treefrogs, *Hyla chrysoscelis*.

◀ The order Caudata contains what are known in broad terms as the salamanders and the newts. In this group one can also find hellbenders, amphiumas, waterdogs, mudpuppies, and sirens. There are about 390 caudate species divided among about eight families. The species depicted is the Large-blotched Salamander, *Ensatina eschscholtzi klauberi*.

➤ Members of the order Caudata (often called "caudates") are characterized by having tails (the very meaning of the word "caudal"), cylindrical elongate bodies, and a distinct head. Most species have limbs that are well-developed, but a handful of the aquatic species (mainly sirens) have reduced limbs that for the most part are unused. The one shown is the Spotted Salamander, *Ambystoma maculatum*.

▶ Although rare in any form of life, bizarre mutations such as that seen on this eight-legged Green Frog, *Rana clamitans*, are particularly rare in amphibians. Most mutants do not live beyond their post-larval stage, if they even get that far.

▶ Amphibians generally are not thought of as fossorial (burrowing) animals, but some are. One of the many advantages to disappearing beneath the earth's surface is that an animal can effectively hide itself until an unsuspecting prey item comes by. It is also a means of escaping predators, plus, some species feed underground as well.

➡ Amphibians probably are not thought of by many as being "intelligent" creatures, but in truth there are quite a few species that have demonstrated a number of rudimentary mental abilities not usually attributed to herptiles.

The anuran skeleton is a fascinating piece of natural engineering. It had to be heavily modified when these creatures turned away from their aquatic world and came on land. The vertebrae became more compact to assist in locomotion and the skull and jaws changed to benefit the capturing of more active prey items. ▶

Shown is the European Toad, *Bufo viridis*.

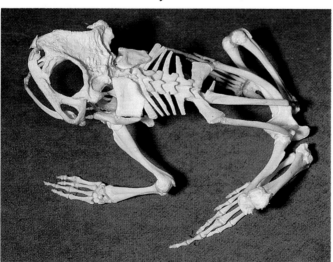

WHAT IS AN AMPHIBIAN?

By the very meaning of the word, "amphibian" means *leading a double life*, and is derived from the Greek *amphibios*. This aptly describes these fascinating creatures—they truly have two aspects of their lives: the aquatic aspect and the terrestrial aspect. Of course, not all the species are locked into this lifestyle on an equal basis. Many amphibians are mostly aquatic while others spend virtually all their time on land. By definition, amphibians breathe through their skin, have paired transmission channels in what is called their "middle" ear, and possess pedicellate (having an elongate base) teeth.

Amphibians belong to the class Amphibia, then are broken down into three main orders: Gymnophiona (sometimes referred to as Apoda), containing the caecilians; Caudata (sometimes called Urodela), containing the salamanders; and Anura, containing the frogs and toads. This species is *Hyperolius acutirostris*.

In this cleared and stained specimen of the Pickerel Frog, *Rana palustris*, you can see clearly the elongate bones of the frog's rear legs and feet. These skeletal details developed so the animal could leap about, and then land, with greater ease.

◀ *Neoteny* is a word applicable to some salamander species. It means "a condition in which the larval form of a species becomes sexually mature while still retaining most larval features (gill stalks, etc.)." The animal depicted here, known as the Tennessee Cave Salamander, *Gyrinophilus palleucus*, is a neotenic species.

WHAT IS AN AMPHIBIAN?

Most amphibians need to keep their skin moist in order to survive, particularly members of the Caudata (salamanders) and the Gymnophiona (caecilians). Some anurans can survive in very dry situations, then others, like this *Xenopus laevis*, lead totally aquatic lives and thus do not venture onto land at all. ▶

Some amateur herpetologists are unaware that the amphiumas, mudpuppies, sirens, hellbenders, and waterdogs are all salamanders that simply have different common names. Most of these creatures are strongly aquatic, have remarkably slippery bodies, and are generally nocturnal. The one shown is the Alabama Waterdog, *Necturus alabamensis.* ▶

◀ Frog and toads are generally regarded as the most specialized amphibians. There are currently about 3800 accepted species divided among about 20 families. It is sometimes very difficult to accurately classify the frogs and toads because of the enormous variety involved. Shown is *Litoria caerulea.*

Many amphibian species are very small, some barely growing over an inch in length. It goes without saying that such creatures are very delicate and can be maintained only with the utmost attention to detail. In the general sense, amphibians are very small creatures overall; only some of the Asian salamander species might be considered "large." ▶

CAECILIANS

Of the three main "groups" of amphibians, the caecilians, of the order Gymnophiona [Apoda], are undoubtedly the most poorly known and least studied. Currently, there are six accepted families occurring in Asia, Africa, and tropical America. Some species can grow to a length of up to 1.5 m/4.95 ft, but most species only reach under half of that. Superficially they look like large earthworms, albeit colorful ones, and are surprisingly easy to keep in captivity provided of course their tanks are kept clean and they are supplied with lots of small vertebrate and invertebrate foods (earthworms, millipedes, etc.).

▶ Some caecilian species, like this model of an *Ichthyophis* sp., are viviparous (giving birth to live young) while others are oviparous (egg-layers). In the latter case it has been found, most interestingly, that if the eggs are removed from the mother they will not develop correctly.

➤ The eyes and ears of the caecilians have regressed so much during the course of evolution that their olfactory senses have become predominant along with two small tentacle-like organs that project from a closable pit on either cheek. In one family, Typhlonectidae, the eyes are still vaguely visible and presumably used for nothing more than light detection. Shown is *Scolecomorphus kirki*.

➤ Although it is easy to get the impression caecilians are rarely seen in the hobby, they do in fact turn up in pet stores with some frequency; particularly

Typhlonectes natans, shown here. The problem is that they are almost always placed with the fishes rather than the herptiles. Their tanks are also often mislabeled as well: "fish eel," "congo eel," "rubber eel," and even the "hosepipe fish."

▶ Speaking in terms of habitat, and from a keeper's point of view, there are two types of caecilians—those that should be kept in an aquarium (aquatic setup) and those that are best kept in a paludarium (half-land half-water setup). You should always know which type you are dealing with before setting up your tank. The species shown here, *Dermophis mexicanus*, would be a paludarium specimen.

◀ Some caecilians can be found in soft, moist terrestrial areas where they will lead a largely fossorial (burrowing) existence. Their known habitats include cultivated fields, termite mounds, humus piles, and so forth. Even an amateur can provide similar surroundings in captivity without going to much trouble. Shown is *Dermophis mexicanus*.

▶ The terrestrial caecilian varieties are probably not seen in the hobby as often as those that are aquatic. This Yellow-striped Caecilian, *Ichthyophis kohtaoensis*, is a land-dweller from Thailand. It does well in a tank bedded with moist potting soil and a well-filtered water body. It can be fed crickets, mealworms, and earthworms. It is also worth noting that the level of moisture must be kept high since these animals dry up fairly easily.

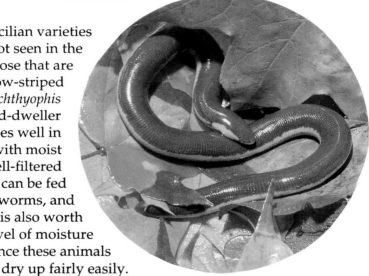

◀ Caecilians don't really have "tails" per se because their cloacal region is located at the terminus of the body. In some species the cloaca could be called subterminal, but only to such a small degree that any length of tail is considered negligible. This is the tail-end of *Typhlonectes natans* .

THE "ODDBALLS"

There are, as we have already discussed, three orders of amphibians—the caecilians (Apoda), frogs and toads (Anura), and salamanders (Caudata). In this third group there are nine families, and some contain animals with most unusual names—hellbenders, waterdogs, and amphiumas, just to name a few. Only advanced hobbyists keep such creatures and often the knowledge of their life histories is very sparse.

◀ There are a number of subterranean salamanders that, for the most part, are totally alien to the hobby of herpetology; this Georgia Blind Salamander, *Haideotriton wallacei*, is a good example. It is known only from a well and a few caves in southwestern Georgia and nearby Florida.

The Dwarf Siren, of the monotypic (containing only one species) genus *Pseudobranchus*, is only occasionally seen in the herpetological hobby. Dwarf Sirens can be found laced about many aquatic plants, particularly the introduced hyacinth *Eichhornia*. Within them the Dwarf Siren will find both secure shelter and a great variety of food items. ◀

◀ Although the process of identifying herptiles is, for some people, very difficult, delineating the three amphiuma species is easy—count their toes. *Amphiuma pholeter* has only one, *A. means* has two, and *A. tridactylum* has three, which is unsurprising since *tridactylum* is Latin for "three-toed."

THE "ODDBALLS"

- The mudpuppies and the waterdogs of the genus *Necturus* are considered "neotenic" animals, meaning they never develop in structure beyond their larval stage and yet still mature sexually and reproduce. One characteristic of larval salamanders is the presence of gill stalks, which can be clearly seen on this Mudpuppy, *Necturus maculosus*.

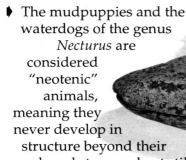

- Amphiumas belong to the "giant salamander" family Amphiumidae, members of which can only be found in North America. There are three amphiuma species, all with slick, darkly colored bodies and vestigial limbs that are for the most part useless. All amphiumas seem to do well in captivity, but many specimens are very nasty and will not hesitate to bite.

The Greater Siren, *Siren lacertina*, occurs from Washington, D.C. south into Florida and then west just out of the Florida Panhandle into Alabama. It is a nocturnal creature that haunts shallow, plant-filled water bodies searching for both soft-bodied invertebrates as well as small shellfish. It is worth noting that the Greater Siren also inadvertently consumes a great deal of plant matter during its feedings. ◄

The Hellbender, *Cryptobranchus alleganiensis*, is very likely the most bizarre and primitive-looking member of the order Caudata. It has a flat body with skin that looks too large for the frame it is wrapped around. It can be found in quick-moving streams where it spends its time hidden under large rocks or other similar shelter (like sunken debris). it is a very slimy creature and therefore difficult to grab.

THE AMPHIBIAN DIET

Amphibians are known as *carnivorous* creatures, meaning quite simply that they consume living flesh. In the wild, an amphibian's diet depends largely on what it can find, but for the most part amphibians feed on the same items—invertebrates such as insects, spiders, and worms, and in the case of some of the larger species, fish and even mice. The key to keeping an amphibian in good health in captivity is not to give it *lots* of food, but a *variety* of food. In fact, variety in the diet is pretty much the key with most herptiles overall. When keeping amphibians in the home, you can assure this variety in the obvious way—by supplying a number of different food items—and also by including the occasional vitamin supplement as well.

◀ As you can tell by this photograph of a *Gyrinophilus* sp. eating a *Plethodon* sp., some amphibian species are cannibalistic. In fact, it would be closer to the truth to say many are, because there are indeed a number of frogs and toads that will gladly gulp down smaller anurans. This is a valuable piece of information to know when deciding which amphibians to house together.

This piece of artwork may seem to exaggerate the anuran diet slightly, but there is some truth to it. The animal depicted is a horned frog of the genus *Ceratophrys*, and accurately illustrates the remarkable voraciousness of the frogs in this genus. ➡

➡ Waxworms are occasionally sold in pet stores and make a fairly good supplement for amphibians, but they are by no means nutritionally complete and should at least be sprinkled with a vitamin powder before they are offered. Furthermore, some keepers consider them a little on the fattening side and choose not to offer them at all.

THE AMPHIBIAN DIET

The poison frogs (members of the family Dendrobatidae) are very popular in the hobby of herpetology, but some specimens can be very difficult to feed. Often a keeper of these tiny amphibians will have to culture wingless fruitflies. As with waxworms and mealworms, these also should occasionally be covered with a vitamin powder. Shown is *Epipedobates tricolor*. ◗

◀Mealworms are an amphibian keeper's delight for many reasons. They are very inexpensive, can be cultured without too much trouble, and are available from a great number of sources. The problem is they do not contain enough nutrients to be an amphibian's sole food.

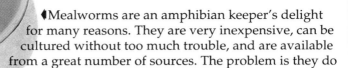

◗ There aren't too many amphibians that will take manufactured foods, but highly aquatic frogs like this Surinam Toad, *Pipa pipa*, will. I sustained one specimen for many years on, among other things, shrimp pellets. These amphibians are usually very willing feeders and will respond to a number of foods.

What do larval salamanders eat? Good question. Some, like the developing Northern Crested Newt, *Triturus cristatus*, shown here, will gladly take bloodworms from a worm cup. Other items include springtails, tubifex worms, and hatchling crickets. ◗

AMPHIBIANS AS PETS

How do amphibians fare in the home? That is a question most budding herpetologists and/or herpetoculturists ask themselves at one point or another. Seeing as how virtually all amphibians are dependent on moist surroundings, one might easily assume they are very delicate and make terrible captives. While that is true in the case of some species, with others it is not. In fact, many amphibians hold remarkable longevity records and could even be termed "hardy." It all depends, of course, on the willingness of the keeper to do what's necessary. In truth, most amphibians need to be given a lot of attention to detail, so if you're not willing to provide this then perhaps they aren't for you.

Small tropical frogs have become very sought-after over the last decade, at least in the West. Shown here is a *Mantella* sp.

The horned frogs of the genus *Ceratophrys* are undoubtedly among the most commonly kept amphibians in today's hobby. They are stout, warty little blobs with a wide mouth and almost a "paisley"-type pattern. Small specimens (about the size of a quarter) will gladly take small crickets and mealworms, then as they grow to adult size they will begin accepting good-sized items like large mice.

Most amphibian species will not allow you to hold them, as I am doing with this Marbled Salamander, *Ambystoma opacum*, and that is an important rule for a keeper to remember. Some amphibians have toxic skin secretions (poison frogs, for example) and others are so slippery that you won't be able to get a grip on them in the first place.

AMPHIBIANS AS PETS

● Treefrogs are very popular with hobbyists and so they should be; they have a lot going for them. For one thing, most varieties available commercially are relatively inexpensive. Furthermore, the captive requirements of treefrogs are not overly demanding and they seem to have a voracious appetite.

The Red-eyed Treefrog, *Agalychnis callidryas*, has enjoyed a great deal of commercial popularity.

Crickets often are considered the "standard" food item for amphibians. There aren't many amphibian species that won't accept crickets of one size or another, and crickets are not only available all year long, they also are quite inexpensive and even easy to breed.

← Metal clips are commonly used as a security measure in conjunction with tank tops, particularly where snakes are concerned, but with amphibians such implements usually are not needed. Of course, when dealing with any kind of captive reptile or amphibian there is always the need for some security, but actually "locking" a tank shut usually is unnecessary.

For terrestrial amphibians, a simple terrarium setup like the one shown here will do very nicely. A tank of this size (20-gallon "long") may seem a little too large for something as small as the Spotted Salamander, *Ambystoma maculatum*, sitting on the piece of bark at the far left corner, but the animal will greatly appreciate the room. ▼

A FROG OR A TOAD?

A question that occasionally comes up in conversation between laymen concerning anurans is "What really is the difference between frogs and toads?" The problem is that the terms "frog" and "toad" don't really have such strict applications that an answer can be given easily. If you wanted to put it in taxonomic terms, the family Ranidae contains what are known as the "true frogs," and the family Bufonidae contains the "true toads," but even those terms are somewhat nebulous.

◀ It is generally believed that most toads dwell on the ground and are large, plump creatures. Species such as this *Bufo atacamensis* have the "standard" toad appearance, complete with the husky build and granular skin.

To demonstrate how unreliable the terms "frog" and "toad" really are, one simply has to use this *Scaphiophryne* sp. as an example. It bears many of the typical toad characteristics— heavy build, warty skin, etc.—but is usually called a "frog" in common English. ▶

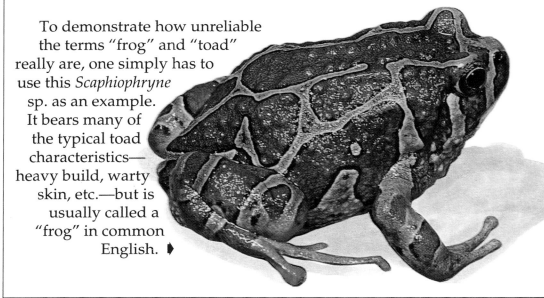

A FROG OR A TOAD?

◀ It would be safe to say frogs are much more inclined to being climbers than toads are. There are, in fact, quite a number of frog genera that are almost exclusively tree-dwelling, including the aptly named "treefrogs," family Hylidae. Shown is *Hyla femoralis*.

◀ Many people believe it is safe to lump frogs and toads into two simple categories—toads having a "warty skin," and frogs have a "smooth skin." While this is true to a degree, there are always exceptions. The skin of this *Bufo typhonius* is fairly granular, but not as pronounced as that of most others of its genus.

One common line people draw between frogs and toads is based on the amount of moisture in their natural habitat. Frogs are supposedly creatures of much wetter locales whereas toads frequent drier communities, but even this rule is not completely sound. This Fire-bellied Toad, *Bombina orientalis*, for example, is an occupant of standing water bodies. ▶

◀ All in all, there are no hard and fast rules as to what the differences are between frogs and toads. It is always best to take an extra moment to find out which term is being used with the animal you are curious about at the time. Also, common names occasionally change. This Asian Spadefoot Toad, *Megophrys monticola*, for example, could one day be called the Asian Spadefoot Frog.

17

REPRODUCTION

The reproductive biology of the anurans is so varied in detail and so fascinating to witness that the topic has intrigued thousands of hobbyists and scientists alike. The reproductive cycle begins at various times of the year, depending on the geographic location of the species in question, with the male and the female locking together in what is known as an "amplexus" position (almost always in water). Eggs can be fertilized either internally or externally, depending on the species, and the young will go through an aquatic larval stage before finally metamorphosing.

◆ Most frog and toad species will experience an aquatic "tadpole" stage in which they have no legs (these will develop later on), breathe through external gills, have a thin laterally flattened rudder-like tail, and possess a disc around the mouth that allows them to adhere to solid objects. Shown is the tadpole of the Green Frog, *Rana clamitans*.

◆ The female of this species, *Rhinophrynus dorsalis*, located on the bottom, is obviously much larger than the male. This often is the case with amphibians. Other external characteristics for sexual dimorphism include swollen folds of skin around the female's cloaca during breeding season and dark, horny toe pads appearing on the males of some species.

◆ Amplexus is the term applied to the standard mating positions used by frogs and toads, but there are different kinds of amplexus as well. Generally speaking, two basic types are recognized—*axillary*, where the male grabs on to the female just behind her front limbs; and *inguinal*, where the grip is placed just above the hindlimbs. These two Wood Frogs, *Rana sylvatica*, are demonstrating axillary amplexus.

REPRODUCTION

◀ A fascinating behavioral aspect of anuran parental care is the carrying of tadpoles on one parent's back. Studies suggest that this is done as both a defensive tactic (bringing the tadpoles out of areas where the adult senses danger) and to introduce the tadpoles to a new food source when their former supply has been depleted. The species shown is *Dendrobates pictus*.

◀ Egg masses often are laid on plant leaves suspended above a water body. The eggs shown here belong to the Red-eyed Treefrog, *Agalychnis callidryas*, from Central America. These eggs will sit for a few days on the leaf and then gradually slide down into the water beneath for further development.

The time of year at which anurans breed depends almost exclusively on their locality. In the north, frogs and toads, along with most other herptiles, will mate in the spring, but in warmer, more tropical climes where the winter month aren't as cold, anurans will begin their cycle considerably earlier. These are two Barking Treefrogs, *Hyla gratiosa*. ▶

REPRODUCTION

Although caudates other than newts have been only marginally popular in the herpetological hobby (compared to, say, snakes and lizards), certain species have been bred in captivity, some through a number of generations. The exact procedure for salamander and newt reproduction of course varies from species to species, but, in general, there is a short ritual of sorts in which the male finds a mate, followed by the male's release of a semen-bearing structure called a "spermataphore" that is picked up by the female for internal fertilization, then the laying of eggs, and finally the hatching of those eggs into tiny larval caudates.

← As is the case with so many other herptiles, most young salamanders do not precisely resemble their parents but instead must grow into that particular appearance. This tiny Marbled Salamander, *Ambystoma opacum*, shows virtually no trace of the attractive silver and black coloration of the parent next to it.

← When two animals of differing species breed and produce offspring it is called *hybridization*. This occurs occasionally in the case of salamanders and newts. This Tremblay's Salamander, *Ambystoma X tremblayi*, for example, comes from the pairing of Jefferson's Salamander, *Ambystoma jeffersonianum*, and the Blue-spotted Salamander, *Ambystoma laterale*. Most interestingly, all *tremblayi* are female. The capital "X" before the species name indicates a hybrid.

REPRODUCTION

Parental protection of salamander eggs has been recorded in many species and indicates a remarkably advanced maternal sense. Some caudates will guard their eggs against predators, others will remain in the nests in order to assure that the eggs become properly moistened (to assure efficient development) by rainfall and flooding, and others may even stay near their eggs until the larvae hatch out completely. Shown is the Mountain Dusky Salamander, *Desmognathus ochrophaeus*.

Members of the genus *Pleurodeles* have a most atypical pre-mating ritual. When a male is ready, he will slide himself under the female and rub the top of his head under her throat, then grab her arms from below. Eventually he will release a spermatophore near the female's head, which she will have to move to receive with her cloacal lips; a process necessary for internal fertilization to occur.

The gill stalks protruding from the posterior portion of a salamander's head are, in most cases, a sign that the salamander in question is in its larval stage, as in the case of this Tiger Salamander, *Ambystoma tigrinum*. It is through these gill stalks that the larvae will breathe. Some aquatic species retain these stalks into adulthood.

Captive salamander and newt breeding is an affair best left to advanced keepers. It is not so much the care of the young that poses the problem, but providing the adults with the correct environment needed to encourage a breeding response. This is the larva of the Long-toed Salamander, *Ambystoma macrodactylum*.

METAMORPHOSIS

Metamorphosis is the process that changes an amphibian from its larval form into the first stages of its adult form. Most amphibians will experience metamorphosis, but some don't. Those that don't are called *neotenous* species and will remain larval throughout their lives (although they will, obviously, still be able to reproduce). Metamorphosis in amphibians is governed by a hormone called *thyroxine* that is further controlled by another called *thyreotropin*. The process of metamorphosis can last anywhere from a few days to a number of months, depending on the species.

➡ The most obvious changes a larval amphibian will experience, at least to the human eye, are morphological ones. During a frog's tadpole stage, for example, it won't look like much more than a small head with a tail attached to it. But as time passes the creature will sprout legs like this *Osteopilus septentrionalis* has, and, in almost all cases, lose the tail completely.

➡Caudate metamorphosis is fascinating although somewhat more subtle than anuran metamorphosis. The overall body shape of most caudates will remain more or less the same from late larva to adult, but there will be some differences. Crests on the back and tail may become smaller or disappear entirely, for example, but the shape of the head will stay essentially the same. Shown here is a mother Marbled Salamander, *Ambystoma opacum*, with a clutch of freshly laid eggs. Interestingly, this species will lay the eggs terrestrially in dry depressions and stay with them until the autumnal rains arrive to flood the depression and release the larvae from the eggs.

METAMORPHOSIS

▶ The Axolotl, *Ambystoma mexicanum*, is perhaps the most well-known example of a neotenic species, at least in the order Caudata. Strongly resembling the larval form of the Tiger Salamander, *Ambystoma tigrinum*, the Axolotl will remain aquatic throughout its natural life. It has, however, been "forced" through full metamorphosis in laboratories by use of heavy exposure to iodine, influencing thyroxine production. The Axolotl is considered a "pedomorphic" animal, meaning it retains many of its juvenile characteristics after becoming sexually mature.

It should be obvious from this photo that some newly metamorphosed anurans are remarkably tiny. To further illustrate this point, it should be noted that the species shown is the Marine Toad, *Bufo marinus*, also known as the Giant Toad because of its relatively huge size—up to 7 in/18 cm (record over 9 in/23 cm). ➤

This intriguing photo shows the egg of a Common Newt, *Triturus vulgaris*, with a clear image of the developing embryo inside. Females of this species usually lay their eggs on submerged plant leaves, then curl the leaves around the eggs to protect them. ➤

➤ The laterally compressed tail is a characteristic shared by almost all larval salamanders, but in many species this trait will not carry over into adulthood. Coloration and pattern will change as well. The mature form of this *Eurycea longicauda*, for example, will be a rich coppery brown with a black dorsal stripe.

MODIFICATIONS

Through the course of evolution, amphibians have developed certain morphological features that allow them to survive better in their natural surroundings. Some of these features, commonly called "modifications," have developed for a whole array of purposes, including defense, offense, breeding, and so on. It would be safe to say every single animal on earth, including man, has modifications, and it is generally accepted that many more will appear through the long passage of time.

◄ An animal's morphological structure will be altered through the course of evolution. In the case of this Lesser Siren, *Siren intermedia*, for example, hind limbs have been lost because there was virtually no need for them.

The vocal sacs of male frogs and toads, like the one seen on this *Bufo cristatus*, are among the most well-known amphibian modifications. They have very thin, very elastic walls and can be singular or paired. These sacs, also known as "gular pouches," are used for mate-calling during the breeding season. ►

◄ The poison frogs, of the family Dendrobatidae, are fairly well-known for their toxic skins, but other amphibians have toxic skin as well, although most of these are not harmful to humans. Such substances were developed as a defense against predators, making the amphibians a distasteful, rather than hearty, meal. Shown is *Dendrobates tinctorius*.

MODIFICATIONS

◀ The toe pads of treefrogs are a fascinating physical modification. A combination of fibers and adhesive secretions allows these creatures to literally "stick" to solid surfaces. When the animal's weight pulls on the toes, fibers automatically squeeze the glands which contain the adhesive substance. Smaller specimens, like this *Centrolenella fleischmanni*, equipped with toe pads can stick to a vertical surface for hours.

Most of the more dramatic amphibian stances are simple defense mechanisms designed to ward off possible predators. In some species, the animal will simply rise up on all fours and perhaps even open its mouth. Other frogs, like this Tomato Frog, *Dyscophus antongili*, will inflate their bodies until they are grossly distorted. ◀

◀ The coloration and patterning of many amphibians is based on that animal's natural environment and is most useful for camouflage when hiding from predators. It is also an offensive advantage as well—these frogs will lay in wait for prey items and go virtually unseen, such as this glass frog, *Hyalinobatrachium* sp.

The hind legs of frogs and toads are elongated and very strong, which aids in their jumping ability. The front legs are short and, in many species, very stout, enabling them to absorb the shock of landing. It is thought by many that larger frogs and toads have a harder time executing this function and consequently cannot cover as great a distance per leap as those species that are more slender and agile, but this simply is not the case. The species shown is *Megophrys aceras*. ◀

25

ANURANS IN CAPTIVITY

Frogs and toads have been kept in captivity for many decades, but only in the last few years have they really begun to enjoy what might be called a "popularity." Herpetoculturists in Europe have developed great skill in keeping anuran species, breeding and raising many for the very first time. In the United States, reptiles are undoubtedly the prevailing entity, but there have been signs pointing to a rise in frog and toad popularity, particularly many of the tropical species; probably due to their beautiful coloration and wide availability.

◄ The treefrogs, family Hylidae, are among the most often-kept anurans. Even for the most exotic species a keeper can expect a reasonable price. Hylids also have relatively undemanding climatic requirements and are very willing to eat. The species shown here is *Hyla regilla*.

◄ A vaguely defined group of anurans that might be termed "micro-frogs" consists of a number of hobby-popular genera, including *Dendrobates*, *Phyllobates*, and *Mantella*, one species of which, *Mantella expectata*, is shown here. It will not grow over 1.5 in/3.8 cm in length.

❯ The "micro-frogs" get their group name from their small size. This trait makes them easy to house since only small tanks are needed. Hypothetically, a keeper could maintain a half-dozen micro-frogs like the *Mantella* sp. depicted here in a 30-gallon tank without worrying about over-crowding.

ANURANS IN CAPTIVITY

◀ The poison frogs, family Dendrobatidae, have long been very popular in the hobby of herpetology. Occurring in Central and South America, these tiny anurans must be kept in moist, humid terraria and maintained on a diet of wingless fruitflies and tiny crickets. This pretty specimen is *Dendrobates trivittatus*.

Unlike some other herptiles, most frogs and toads are willing and eager feeders. The staple diet for most species is probably insects, but some, like this *Pyxicephalus adspersus*, grow large enough to eat small mice. ◄

For people who keep large numbers of frogs and toads, simple tank setups probably are best. A tank filled with plants and soil may look nice, but if you have a large number of tanks, keeping them clean will become very tiresome and laborious. If you use gravel, as in the case with the micro-frogs shown here, be sure there is enough water on the tank floor to maintain the proper amount of moisture. ▶

CAUDATES IN CAPTIVITY

Of all the major groups of herptiles kept in today's hobby—snakes, lizards, turtles, frogs and toads, and salamanders and newts—the last group is probably the least popular. Why? That's hard to say. In truth, they are actually wonderful terrarium, aquarium, and paludarium subjects with fascinating behaviors and life habits. It is a myth that most salamander and newt species refuse to eat (they, in fact, are very willing feeders if given the proper surroundings and food of appropriate size), but it is not a myth that they spend most of their time in hiding, which is not much fun for the keeper who wants to admire his or her pets. On a more positive note, they occur in a number of beautiful color and pattern varieties and when they are seen for sale some are quite inexpensive.

◀ Members of the family Ambystomatidae, such as the Mole Salamander, *Ambystoma talpoideum*, shown here, have garnered a reputation for being hardy, dependable captives. Their feeding requirements are very undemanding, and some species are strikingly pretty. They even have been captive-bred through a number of generations.

◀ This photo shows the proper way to grasp a salamander in the event that a keeper ever feels the need to do so. In reality, salamanders and newts do not like being held and usually will squirm about until they are released. The species I am holding here is a Marbled Salamander, *Ambystoma opacum*.

CAUDATES IN CAPTIVITY

▶ Newts, like this attractive little Alpine Newt, *Triturus alpestris*, probably are the most often-sold members of the order Caudata. They are lively little creatures that can be kept in a mostly aquatic tank (with a small land body or floating platform for basking) and will eat small invertebrates.

◀ Some salamander and newt species probably are best avoided by the amateur simply because most specimens have displayed such poor adaptability to captivity. The Red Salamander, *Pseudotriton ruber*, is a good example of this type of animal.

◀ In the case of largely terrestrial species, such as this Marbled Salamander, *Ambystoma opacum*, many keepers prefer to provide little or no water at all. However, every salamander and newt should be given at least a small body of water.

◀ Collecting herpetological specimens from the wild certainly is one method for building a collection, but in the case of salamanders and newts you may be in for a real challenge. Most caudates occur in wet, mucky regions like the one shown here and are very adept at hiding.

ALBINISM AND MELANISM

There is a popular aspect of today's herpetological hobby whose main point of appeal deals with albinistic and melanistic reptile and amphibian specimens. Snakes are undoubtedly the leader in this area, and then turtles. But what about amphibians? And what exactly is albinism and melanism? In brief, albinism is the result of a gene's failure to produce a pigment called melanin, which gives an animal its dark brown or black coloration. In the reverse situation an overabundance of melanin is produced, creating a very dark or melanistic animal.

◄ A beautiful albino specimen of the Bullfrog, *Rana catesbeiana*. Note the light coloration of the eyes—even there the dark pigmentation is absent.

◄ Two examples of the same species, *Ambystoma maculatum*, the Spotted Salamander, showing the remarkable difference between an albino specimen (top) and a normal one (bottom). Note how the lighter colors remain completely unchanged. Albino salamanders are very rare.

ALBINISM AND MELANISM

The reason albino herptiles, like this *Rana temporaria*, rarely are found in the wild is because their outstanding appearance makes them easy targets for predators. The colors of a normal animal usually will blend into the natural environment making it hard to see, but one that has been stripped of this camouflage will be much more susceptible to attack. ▶

◀ As in albinism, so are there degrees of melanism. In some cases the animal appears completely black, patterns and colors having been totally obscured. In others, like this Marbled Salamander, *Ambystoma opacum*, vague traces remain.

Albino amphibians appear rarely on the commercial market and even in those cases they are remarkably expensive. This albino Tiger Salamander, *Ambystoma tigrinum*, is a captive-bred adult and represents perhaps only a handful of albino Tiger Salamanders worldwide. ▶

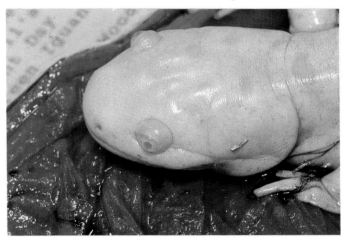

There is a belief that albino herptiles can have unpredictable temperaments compared to normally colored specimens. In some cases, an animal generally considered calm will bite viciously and never tame down. This remarkable albino Argentine Horned Frog, *Ceratophrys ornata*, which I saw in Orlando, Florida, was like that. ▶

POISON FROGS

The family Dendrobatidae includes several frogs that are among the most colorful and fascinating of all amphibians. Formerly called "poison-arrow" or "poison-dart" frogs, they get their collective name from the fact that some South American indians coat the tips of their blowgun darts with the poisons a few of these tiny frogs secrete from their skins. In some instances the chemical makeup of these poisons is used to distinguish one species from another. Most dendrobatids occur in northern South America, but their range also extends into Central America as well.

◀ *Dendrobates auratus* appears in over a dozen different color varieties, and even varies in size depending on the geographical origin of the specimen. It can be found in cocoa plantations in Panama and northwestern Colombia and reaches a maximum adult length of almost 2.5 in/6.4 cm. Specimens in the hobby largely descend from ancestors in a population introduced into Hawaii decades ago.

◀ Unquestionably one of the most stunning of all the poison frogs, *Dendrobates azureus* (the Blue Poison Frog) is rare in the wild although it is becoming popular with hobbyists. It lives mostly on the ground near jungle streams in a very small sector of Surinam.

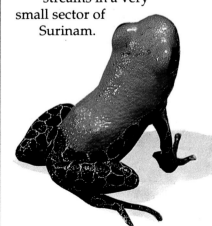

◀ *Dendrobates reticulatus* is one of the more commonly seen dendrobatids in the herpetological hobby. It is one of the smallest of this already very small group, rarely growing beyond 0.6 in/1.5 cm, and requires a humidity level in the upper 80's to lower 90's in captivity.

POISON FROGS

◀ The color of *Dendrobates quinquevittatus* varies from population to population, five different general forms being recognized in all. This one, with the bold stripes and reticulated legs, probably comes from somewhere near French Guyana.

Epipedobates is one of the "newer" genera of poison arrow frogs, being first suggested by Myers in 1987. This familiar species is known as *Epipedobates tricolor*. It occurs in Ecuador at heights of well over 4000 ft/1220 m above sea level. ▶

◀ A very attractive and diminutive creature, *Dendrobates histrionicus* has not, unlike many other dendrobatids, been successfully bred in numbers in captivity. The degree of difficulty involved in breeding dendrobatid frogs varies from species to species.

Parental care of the eggs and young of the poison frogs is well-known. One of the most intriguing examples of this behavior is the way *Dendrobates pumilio* nourishes its offspring by producing special eggs, known as "food eggs," that the tadpoles feed upon. ▶

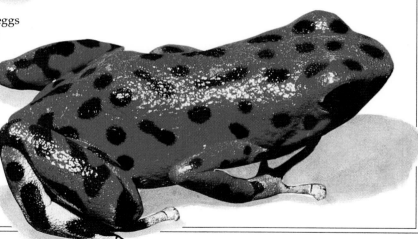

MORE POISON FROGS

Perhaps the most fascinating aspect of the poison frogs is their sometimes strange but always intriguing behavior. Take, for instance, the territorial instincts of the males. In captivity, some males have been known to actually kill those of other species in order to preserve and defend an area they have considered to be their own. Furthermore, studies have shown that it takes a male poison frog that has been placed in a new locale only about an hour to decide it is his.

▶ Occurring in damp lowland regions on the Pacific coast of Costa Rica, *Dendrobates granuliferus* has been collected for many years for the herpetological hobby. It is a long-lived captive but successfully propagating the species is difficult because the young have a highly specialized diet.

◀ Telling the dendrobatid sexes apart can be very difficult because external morphological characteristics are either very subtle or completely nonexistent. In some male specimens of *Dendrobates pumilio*, however, there will be a notable dark patch on the throat.

As with many other dendrobatid species, there are so many different color forms of *Dendrobates pumilio* that one could easily get the impression of looking at a different frog altogether. Often when trying to identify a particular animal, information on exactly where it came from is essential. ➥

➥ Not a great deal is known about the attractive *Dendrobates histrionicus* although it is fairly abundant where it occurs. It is adaptable to both lowland and mountainous regions, where it spends its time in heavy vegetation on the rainforest floor.

➥ Although *Phyllobates lugubris* is not seen all that often on the pet market, it is nevertheless fairly easy to maintain. It will require a tank stuffed with plants and a day/night temperature gradient of between 72 and 82°F (22 and 29°C).

➥ Generally easy to maintain and breed, *Dendrobates leucomelas* is a native of the lowland rainforest regions of Colombia and Venezuela into Guyana and Brazil. It requires a high humidity as well as a high temperature and is fairly cryptic regardless of its diurnal nature.

◄ This is one of the more attractive and interestingly patterned variants of *Dendrobates histrionicus*. It grows to a respectable length for this family—about 1.5 in/3.8 cm—and can be kept in a humid terrarium with relative ease.

FAMILY HYLIDAE

Known in collective terms as the treefrogs, some of the more hobby-popular members of this family include the Red-eyed Treefrog, *Agalychnis callidryas*; the Green Treefrog, *Hyla cinerea*; the marsupial frog, *Gastrotheca*; and the Dumpy Treefrog, *Litoria caerulea*. Most of the hylids are arboreal (tree-dwelling) but a few are terrestrial, semiaquatic, and palustral (marsh-dwelling). Most hylid frogs sold commercially do well in captivity, displaying a great willingness to eat a number of easily obtainable live insects.

For the keeper interested in maintaining hylids, a "high" tank as opposed to a "long" one is a must with virtually every species. Climbers like these *Hyla arborea* will spend most of their time off the ground and would greatly appreciate the inclusion of a few plants, branches, and so forth. ▶

◀ The cricket frogs, genus *Acris*, are among the few hylids that are not climbers. They spend their days foraging for insects and other small invertebrates in and around shallow, vegetated bodies of water. They can occur in very thick populations and will not hesitate to jump away from human observers. The species shown here is *Acris gryllus*.

FAMILY HYLIDAE

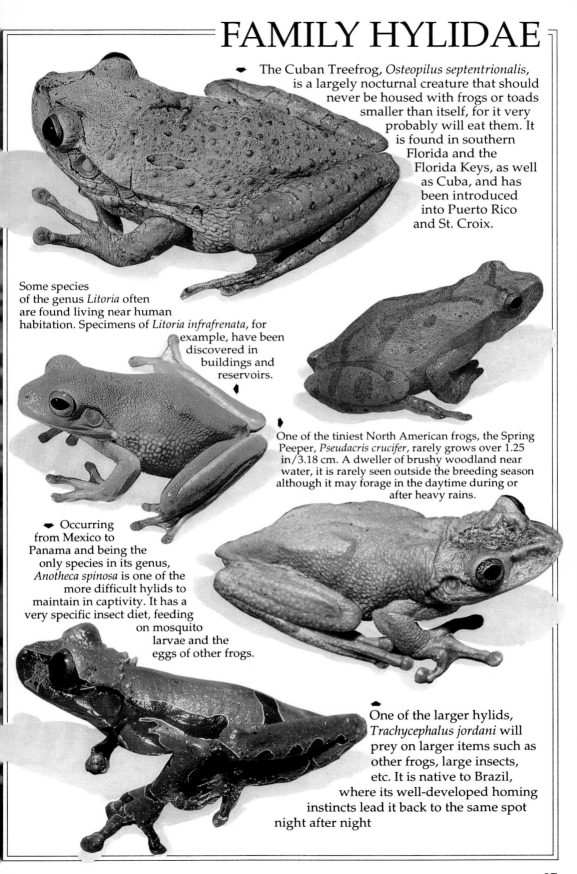

The Cuban Treefrog, *Osteopilus septentrionalis*, is a largely nocturnal creature that should never be housed with frogs or toads smaller than itself, for it very probably will eat them. It is found in southern Florida and the Florida Keys, as well as Cuba, and has been introduced into Puerto Rico and St. Croix.

Some species of the genus *Litoria* often are found living near human habitation. Specimens of *Litoria infrafrenata*, for example, have been discovered in buildings and reservoirs.

One of the tiniest North American frogs, the Spring Peeper, *Pseudacris crucifer*, rarely grows over 1.25 in/3.18 cm. A dweller of brushy woodland near water, it is rarely seen outside the breeding season although it may forage in the daytime during or after heavy rains.

Occurring from Mexico to Panama and being the only species in its genus, *Anotheca spinosa* is one of the more difficult hylids to maintain in captivity. It has a very specific insect diet, feeding on mosquito larvae and the eggs of other frogs.

One of the larger hylids, *Trachycephalus jordani* will prey on larger items such as other frogs, large insects, etc. It is native to Brazil, where its well-developed homing instincts lead it back to the same spot night after night

FAMILY BUFONIDAE

Many people undoubtedly remember the classic claim that touching a toad will give you warts. This, of course, is not only untrue but gives these charming little creatures a bad reputation that is wholly undeserved. Perhaps this myth spawned from the fact that most toads are covered with a warty, granulate skin. Other features that distinguish this family, known as the "true toads," include a stout, heavy body, a horizontally oval pupil, and in many cases an conspicuous paratoid gland extending back from just behind the eye.

◄ The Colorado River Toad, *Bufo alvarius*, has been called "one of the most intelligent of all amphibians." Occurring only in the most southwestern parts of the United States, it is now a popular terrarium pet and grows large enough to eat small mice without difficulty.

▶ A most attractive and fascinating genus, the stub-footed toads, genus *Atelopus*, have a most remarkable embryonic development—the eggs hatch only about 24 hours after they are laid, and the young will fully metamorphose in just a few weeks. With more than 30 species in South and Central America, the stub-foots are very delicate and rarely kept in captivity.

◄ Not much is known about this life history of the Marbled Toad, *Bufo marmoreus*. It was first described in 1833 and is a resident of Mexico. Due to its rather typical bufonid form and unremarkable appearance, it is not regarded by hobbyists and thus does not appear commercially. Nevertheless, it is a hardy animal and an opportunistic feeder in the wild.

FAMILY BUFONIDAE

Found along river banks either on the ground or in the lower reaches of thick vegetation, the Asian tree-toad *Pedostibes hosii* occurs in southern Thailand, Sumatra, and the Kalimantan lowlands. It feeds mainly on ants. The females can display a purplish shading. ▶

Toads of the recently described (1938) genus *Pelophryne* are, as you can see, very bizarre in appearance, particularly in regard to the head. Natives of tropical Southeast Asia, they have a very rapid embryonic and larval growth and live in rain and cloud forest regions. There are about a half-dozen species in the genus, most of them indistinct, and none grow over 1.6 in/4 cm. The species shown is *Pelophryne lemur*. ▶

◀ Native to most of the arid regions of the North American Southwest, the Red-spotted Toad, *Bufo punctatus*, can be found close to seepages, springs, and run-off pools. It breeds during rainy periods from April to September, the males usually calling from rocks rather than from in the water.

FAMILY RANIDAE

Ranids are known collectively as the "true frogs" and are distributed over much of the earth although most species occur in southern Asia and Africa. They are very difficult to pin down in terms of breeding habits and behavioral characteristics due to an enormous degree of variation; this family could be considered sort of a "junk drawer" taxon. There are tree-dwellers, ground-dwellers, and heavily aquatic species. Those that are sold commercially usually do very well.

← Found only on the Solomon Islands, *Ceratobatrachus guentheri* was first described in 1884 and occurs in a variety of colors. It is a highly terrestrial species and rarely seen in the herpetological hobby.

Most of the ranids can be kept comfortable in an aquaterrarium or paludarium (half-land, half-water) with a three- or four-day interval between feedings. The *Rana chaochiaoensis*, shown here, for example, can be kept in this fashion. You should, however, investigate the origin of each specimen you have in order to determine correct temperature. ▸

◂ Perhaps the hardiest of all ranids, the Bullfrog, *Rana catesbeiana*, is also the largest frog in North America—some specimens grow to 6 in/15.2 cm (known record is 8 in/20.3 cm) in body length. It is very quick to jump away from human intruders and therefore is very difficult to capture.

FAMILY RANIDAE

One of the few ranids that does not frequent the water, *Arthroleptis variabilis* is a nocturnal ground-dweller that spawns in moistened soil. In captivity it needs a thick layer of loose substrate material and a fairly high temperature. It will probably spend much of its time burrowed, so a keeper can expect to see an empty tank most of the time. ☙

◄ A fascinating terrarium subject, the African Bullfrog, *Pyxicephalus adspersus*, will spend much of its time burrowed under loose, moist soil, lying in wait for its prey—which can be small mice in the case of larger specimens. It is a bold animal and will not hesitate to bite its keeper.

Frogs in the genus *Cacosternum* vary highly in appearance. There are only five species, but the genus is poorly known and each of those species is fairly indistinct. They can be found in exposed areas near water bodies, especially during the breeding season when they will group in very large numbers. Shown is the Kalahari Dainty Frog, *Cacosternum boettgeri*. ☙

☙ In the more northerly parts of its range, the Wood Frog, *Rana sylvatica*, will have shorter hind legs than those in the South and will hop more like a toad than a ranid. It can be identified by the prominent dark "robber's mask" that runs back from the eye.

FAMILY MICROHYLIDAE

A fairly widely distributed group of frogs, members of the family Microhylidae, otherwise known as the narrow-mouthed toads, can be found over Southeast Asia, the Americas, southern and eastern Africa, and parts of Madagascar. Most spend their time on or in the ground but some tropical species are arboreal. The young often will develop outside water. Interestingly, most species in this group lack teeth and therefore must be given very soft food in captivity. Wingless fruitflies, waxworms and mealworms, tiny crickets, and ants are suggested.

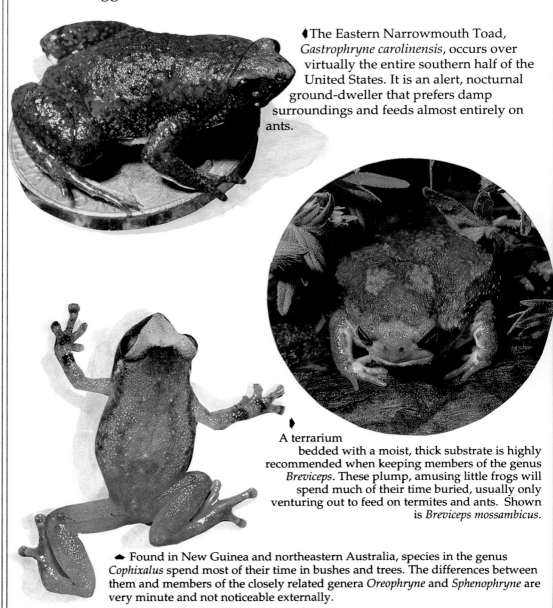

◀The Eastern Narrowmouth Toad, *Gastrophryne carolinensis*, occurs over virtually the entire southern half of the United States. It is an alert, nocturnal ground-dweller that prefers damp surroundings and feeds almost entirely on ants.

A terrarium bedded with a moist, thick substrate is highly recommended when keeping members of the genus *Breviceps*. These plump, amusing little frogs will spend much of their time buried, usually only venturing out to feed on termites and ants. Shown is *Breviceps mossambicus*.

◆ Found in New Guinea and northeastern Australia, species in the genus *Cophixalus* spend most of their time in bushes and trees. The differences between them and members of the closely related genera *Oreophryne* and *Sphenophryne* are very minute and not noticeable externally.

FAMILY MICROHYLIDAE

◀ The Great Plains Narrowmouth Toad, *Gastrophryne olivacea*, can be readily distinguished from other members of its genus by the total (or close to total) lack of patterning. They are residents of fairly dry regions and can sometimes be found sharing burrows with tarantulas.

Members of the genus *Phrynomerus* are known as the "creeping frogs," and with good reason—they do not have any jumping ability. They do, however, usually have very attractive colors and patterns, like those on this *Phrynomerus bifasciatus*, and are therefore sometimes found in the pet trade. They feed eagerly on ants and termites and should be kept in a semi-moist terrarium. ▶

Currently considered one of the most popular anurans in the hobby, the Tomato Frog, *Dyscophus antongili*, is unquestionably well-deserving of its status. Native to tropical northwestern Madagascar, it shows a remarkable adaptability to captive life, a willingness to eat (crickets, etc.), and is known to be quite long-lived. ◀

◀ The round body, pointed snout, and tiny head all are hallmarks of the genus *Dermatonotus*. Occurring only in parts of South America, these unique-looking frogs are virtually never seen in the pet trade although they are known to be fairly hardy. They are primarily terrestrial and feed on ants and termites. This particular species is *Dermatonotus muelleri*.

GENUS *CERATOPHRYS*

An entire chapter on one frog genus? Why not! When we're talking about popular, we're talking about the horned frogs. Some hobbyists keep nothing else, others breed them in huge numbers. They have a lot going for them, after all—good looks, personality, adaptability to captivity, a voracious appetite, etc. There is now, in fact, even a striking albino variety, and although it currently commands a respectable price, it undoubtedly will become more and more available as time passes.

How about a little geographical data? As a whole, the horned frogs can be found in both tropical and subtropical South America east of the Andes Mountains, and some occur on the Pacific and Caribbean coastal regions in the north. This particular species, *Ceratophrys ornata*, is from in southeastern Brazil and northeastern Argentina.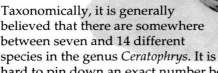

Taxonomically, it is generally believed that there are somewhere between seven and 14 different species in the genus *Ceratophrys*. It is hard to pin down an exact number because of the eternally conflicting opinions among taxonomists. The specimens shown here are both *Ceratophrys cornuta*. ☛

GENUS *CERATOPHRYS*

◄ The plump, stout body is a characteristic of the horned frogs, as is the large head, wide mouth (sometimes more than half the body length), horizontal pupil, heart-shaped tongue, and, of course, the horns above their eyes that give them their collective name. The patterns and colors usually are very ornate, and the skin has a rough, granular texture, which can be seen clearly on this *Ceratophrys calcarata*.

► In captivity, horned frogs are notorious for their voracious appetites. A huge variety of items can be offered to even the very youngest specimens, and in the case of the older "veteran captives," virtually anything will be taken, including small mice, lizards, and strips of raw meat. The species shown is *Ceratophrys aurita*.

► It should be pointed out to keepers of horned frogs that as specimens grow in size, so will their boldness and aggression. When angered, they will not think twice before lashing out at even the most familiar keeper, and due to their sharp teeth a solid bite can be very painful. Shown is *Ceratophrys calcarata*.

Until recently, breeding *Ceratophrys* in captivity was a bit of a mystery. Apparently the act of injecting hormones into healthy adults is required (a larger dose for the females), then they are put together for the actual mating, and then the eggs (numbering as high as 1000) are collected and reared in individual containers because the tadpoles are carnivorous and will not think twice before eating each other. The species shown, *Ceratophrys aurita*, has not, to my knowledge, been bred much if it all. ►

FAMILY AMBYSTOMATIDAE

If I were asked to give an opinion as to which family of salamanders made the best pets, I would, without hesitation, choose this one. Furthermore, I would even say they were among the most interesting as well. You would have to look long and hard to find a more visually compelling group, and their calm nature, relative hardiness, moderate size, and faring in artificial environments only adds to that intrigue. The taxonomic arrangement of the ambystomids is fairly flimsy, although, as with so many other groups of animals, this always seems to be the case.

◀ The largest of the ambystomids, the Tiger Salamander, *Ambystoma tigrinum*, grows to a length of about 8.8 in/22 cm and is an enthusiastic feeder. Captive specimens have been maintained on a mouse diet and lived long, healthy lives. Some specimens, however, have unpredictable tempers and may bite.

➡ Members of the family Ambystomatidae can be found across virtually all of temperate North America (except some of the Southwest and into Baja) including much of northern Mexico. This particular species, *Ambystoma subsalsum* (considered by some to be a synonym of *Ambystoma tigrinum*), was first found in a small crater lake in eastern Puebla, Mexico.

Undoubtedly one of the most stunning members of the family, *Ambystoma cingulatum*, also known as the Flatwoods Salamander, spends much of its time hiding under objects near cypress swamps in slashpine woodland. Growing to just about 5 in/12.7 cm, it is not often seen in the herpetological hobby. ◀

FAMILY AMBYSTOMATIDAE

▶ The Ringed Salamander, *Ambystoma annulatum*, a truly beautiful animal, occurs in Missouri, Arkansas, and Oklahoma, where it congregates in huge numbers during the fall for breeding, almost always following cool rains. It is rarely seen in the hobby since it is protected in almost every part of its range.

One of the most commonly kept ambystomids is the Spotted Salamander, *Ambystoma maculatum*, a reclusive species that occurs over much of the eastern half of the United States. The spotting that gives it its common name can be either yellow or orange, and in rare specimens there is no spotting at all. ◀

◀ A gorgeous example of the Caudata, the Blue-spotted Salamander, *Ambystoma laterale*, is perhaps best-known among professional herpetologists as the salamander that hybridizes heavily with Jefferson's Salamander, *Ambystoma jeffersonianum*, over an enormous area. It breeds in the spring and occurs well into southern Canada.

◀ At 6 in/15.2 cm average adult length, the Pacific Giant Salamander, *Dicamptodon ensatus*, seems to have earned its common name. One of the few ambystomids not in the genus *Ambystoma*, it prefers cool woodland and mountainous areas and has been seen well off the ground's surface, climbing through trees and shrubs. Captors are cautioned not to handle this occasionally vicious and unpredictable species.

FAMILY SALAMANDRIDAE

   Geographically speaking, this family is known as a "quadripartite" group, which, in the English that normal people (non-scientists) speak, means "divided into four parts." There are salamandridids in both eastern and western North America (disjunct), Europe, and central and eastern Asia (conjunct), making them a very widespread clan. They have poison glands in their skin, which is hardly unknown to other salamander families, theirs being the most toxic. As in so many other amphibians, the bright coloration of most species relays their toxicity to would-be predators.

◀ Information on the life history of *Pachytriton brevipes* is not abundant. It occurs in flowing water bodies at the foothills of mountains in southeastern China, where it leads an almost totally aquatic life. It breeds in late summer and the females lay about five dozen eggs. A calm, retiring animal, most specimens will not grow over 6 in/15.2 cm.

Known in the vernacular as the "imperial newts" or "crocodile newts," members of the genus *Tylototriton* can be found in China, northern Southeast Asia, and Japan. They are semi-aquatic and have been bred through many generations in captivity. They are easy to keep, inexpensive, and rather colorful. This species is *Tylototriton verrucosus*. ◀

   Undoubtedly one of the most desirable members of the family Salamandridae, the Northern Crested Newt, *Triturus cristatus*, occurs throughout most of Europe and in northern Anatolia and the Caucasus region. In captivity these animals are best kept in a damp terrarium with a fairly cool temperature, then, during the spring, they should be placed in a mostly aquatic tank. ◀

FAMILY SALAMANDRIDAE

The Rough-skinned Newt, *Taricha granulosa*, can claim its fame as being one of the most poisonous newts in North America. A remarkably bold creature, it lays its eggs singly rather than in a mass, as do the other species of its genus.

Thousands of newts of the genus *Notophthalmus* are sold in pet shops in the United States every year. These spirited little creatures have a lot going for them—they are very inexpensive, fairly hardy, and will eat a variety of food items. The one pictured here, known as the Black-spotted Newt, *Notophthalmus meridionalis*, is one of the lesser-seen species. ▶

The Red-spotted Newt, *Notophthalmus viridescens viridescens*, goes through three phases during its lifetime—the first is an aquatic stage, the second is terrestrial, and the third returns it to the water. During the terrestrial stage it is known as a "Red Eft," a beautiful specimen of which is shown here. ◀

One of the most commonly kept newts, the Fire Salamander, *Salamandra salamandra*, slightly resembles the popular Spotted Salamander, *Ambystoma maculatum*, of North America, at least in coloration and general size. It is a hardy captive (although the lower temperature requirements may be annoying to some keepers) and will eat a variety of small insects. ◀

FAMILY PLETHODONTIDAE

The common name for this family—the "lungless salamanders"—is self-explanatory: members breathe through what is known as "cutaneous respiration," or, in simpler terms, through their skin. These are the only salamanders that reach the Southern Hemisphere. Natural habitats vary enormously, which is not surprising since this is an enormous group. Some can be found in creek beds, others in subterranean streams, a few live on land, and then there are the few that have highly arboreal habits.

◄ An enormous genus containing over 50 species, members of *Bolitoglossa*, can be found from Mexico to Bolivia and Brazil. They range in a wide variety of habitats and many species feed largely on ants. The specimen shown is a *Bolitoglossa dofleini*.

◄ Occurring over a large portion of the eastern United States and further into Canada, the Dusky Salamander, *Desmognathus fuscus*, will spend most of its time hiding under stones and debris on the edges of slow-moving water bodies. There are two subspecies, the second being *D. f. conanti*, named after noted herpetologist Dr. Roger Conant.

◄ The Ensatina, *Ensatina eschscholtzi*, is one of the more colorful members of the Plethodontidae, occurring strictly along the West Coast of the United States and just into Canada. There are a number of currently recognized subspecies. The females, most interestingly, often will care for their eggs in underground cavities.

FAMILY PLETHODONTIDAE

The Zigzag Salamander, *Plethodon dorsalis*, gets its common name from the shape of the light stripe on its back. In some specimens the edges of the stripe are very sharp and well-defined, whereas in others it is very distorted and hardly looks "zigzaggish" at all.

A hardy and lively little salamander, *Batrachoseps attenuatus*, otherwise known as the California Slender Salamander, often will turn up in people's yards! Occurring mainly along the western coast of northern California and just into Oregon, the mothers often will lay their eggs in large communal nests.

Found in cooler and moister regions, the Spring Salamander, *Gyrinophilus porphyriticus*, rarely is seen in the terrarium. Occurring only in the eastern United States, it can be found by turning logs or boards near cool streams or in marshy wetlands. A specimen will not be difficult to spot once it is exposed, however, as it is very striking.

The Clouded Salamander, *Aneides ferreus*, seems to have a strong likeness for Douglas fir forests, where it often can be revealed by tearing the bark from fallen examples of these pretty trees. It is generally presumed that this species breeds during the middle to late winter months, then lays eggs in large nests that are sometimes occupied by both the males and the females.

NORTH AMERICA

For all intents and purposes, the region known as "North America" is comprised of what we know as Canada, the United States, and northern Mexico south into the Mexican Highlands. It would be safe to say North America is more or less completely encased in what is known in zoogeographical terms as the "Nearctic" region. As far as the Amphibia are concerned, there are an astounding number of species, genera, and even families that occur exclusively within North American boundaries. Climate zones range from subtropical to Arctic, which partially explains the diversity of amphibian life.

◀The attractive and fascinating Spring Peepers, *Pseudacris crucifer*, are rarely seen outside the breeding season. Occurring over virtually all of the eastern United States and well into Canada, the pretty trilling sounds of the males can be heard near patches of trees and shrubs that stand in water.

Found mostly in the United States but with representatives also occurring in Canada and Mexico, the genus *Ambystoma* is exclusive to North America. Popular terrarium subjects such as the Axolotl, *A. mexicanum*, and the Tiger Salamander, *A. tigrinum*, are part of this hardy, impressive group. Shown here is the rarely seen California Tiger Salamander, *A. californiense*. ▶

◀ One of the more abundant North American frogs, the Northern Leopard Frog, *Rana pipiens*, often is sold in pet stores, usually for a very low price. A voracious eater, it will not grow over 3.5 in/8.9 cm. Specimens have been found quite a long distance from water, hence their "secondary" name (more like a nickname) the "Meadow" Frogs.

▶ It is appropriate that in a chapter concerned with North America a photo of the American Toad, *Bufo americanus*, be included. A hardy, spunky little beast, it can be found almost anyplace in the Northeast where an abundant supply of small vertebrate and invertebrate foods can be found—even in suburban yards. A long-lived captive, it needs a thick substrate in which to burrow and can keep the company only of others nearest to its own size; it will eat those that are much smaller.

A most confusing little animal, Cope's Treefrog, *Hyla chrysoscelis*, looks so much like its genus-mate the Gray Treefrog, *Hyla versicolor*, that only their voices tell them apart. For a short time they were both given the same common name (Gray) since they are so morphologically similar. ▶

◀ Often seen in captivity, the Smallmouth Salamander, *Ambystoma texanum*, occurs over a fairly large portion of the United States. It varies in pattern from almost totally black to black with heavy silvery speckling. Breeding in the late winter/early spring, it hybridizes with both the Tiger Salamander and Jefferson's Salamander, although only rarely.

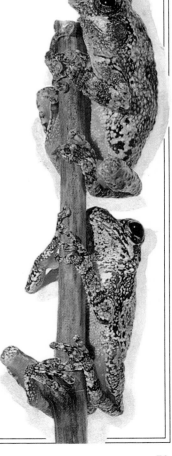

◀ North America is home to a number of newt species. The most popular of these, as far as commercialization is concerned, is probably the Red-spotted Newt, *Notophthalmus viridescens*. A hardy and easily kept captive, it occurs over much of the eastern United States and into Canada.

SOUTH/CENTRAL AMERICA

South and Central America comprise a zoogeographical area known as the Neotropic Region. Bordered in the north by the Nearctic and in the south by the Antarctic, the Neotropics contain some of the most unique and diversified forms of faunal and floral life in the world. A great many herptiles, both reptile and amphibian alike, are imported from South and Central America every year, and it's getting to the point now that this situation should really come to a halt or many species will be threatened by extirpation.

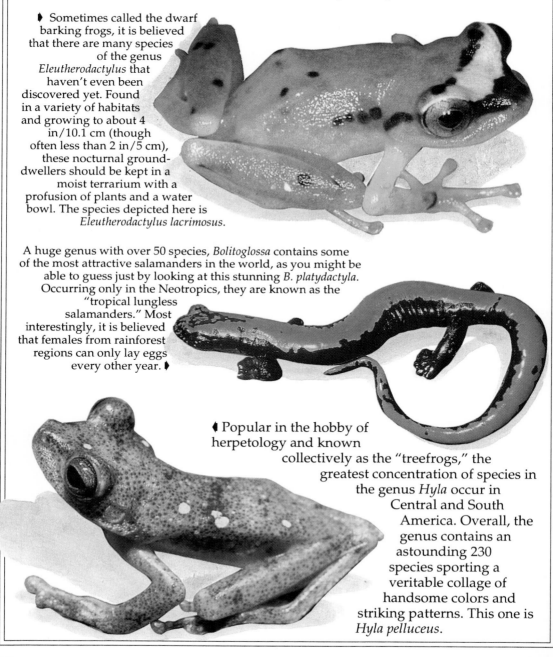

◗ Sometimes called the dwarf barking frogs, it is believed that there are many species of the genus *Eleutherodactylus* that haven't even been discovered yet. Found in a variety of habitats and growing to about 4 in/10.1 cm (though often less than 2 in/5 cm), these nocturnal ground-dwellers should be kept in a moist terrarium with a profusion of plants and a water bowl. The species depicted here is *Eleutherodactylus lacrimosus*.

A huge genus with over 50 species, *Bolitoglossa* contains some of the most attractive salamanders in the world, as you might be able to guess just by looking at this stunning *B. platydactyla*. Occurring only in the Neotropics, they are known as the "tropical lungless salamanders." Most interestingly, it is believed that females from rainforest regions can only lay eggs every other year. ◗

◖ Popular in the hobby of herpetology and known collectively as the "treefrogs," the greatest concentration of species in the genus *Hyla* occur in Central and South America. Overall, the genus contains an astounding 230 species sporting a veritable collage of handsome colors and striking patterns. This one is *Hyla pelluceus*.

◀The enormously popular horned frogs, genus *Ceratophrys*, are residents of South America. A genus containing probably at least a dozen species, members occur in both wet and dry regions and bury most of their bodies in soft soil during daytime or dusk hours waiting for prey—virtually anything they can fit into their mouths—to wander by. The species shown is the Ornate Horned Frog, *C. ornata*.

Very little is known about the reproductive biology of the rare and attractive *Lithodytes lineatus*. Occurring in the outer limits of the Amazon Basin, it bears more than a passing resemblance to many of the poison frogs, family Dendrobatidae. It is known to be active both nocturnally and diurnally and spends virtually all of its time on the ground. ➡

The now-famous poison frogs, family Dendrobatidae, which have caused such a stir in the hobby of herpetology, call South and Central America their home. With over 80 species and at least a half-dozen genera, they are considered by many to be the most visually captivating herptiles in the world. The species you see here, *Epipedobates tricolor*, is currently very popular. ➡

Belonging to one of the few largely arboreal salamander genera, specimens of *Pseudoeurycea* sometimes can be found prowling close to areas of human habitation. The mothers lay fairly small egg clutches (around two dozen) and then guard them until they hatch—as fully metamorphosed young. The species shown, *P. belli*, should be kept in a fairly cool terrarium.
▲

ASIA

Like North America, virtually all of the continent of Asia falls into the zoogeographical category known as the Palerctic Region. Asia is the home to many amphibian species, including a few of the caecilians, order Gymnophiona. Physically, Asia is the largest continent, and the major part of the supercontinent known as Eurasia, which combines it with the considerably smaller Europe. Asia extends north into the Arctic Circle and south almost to the equator, which means it has a vast variety of habitats to offer.

▶ Members of the genus *Tylototriton* can only be found in the eastern Palearctic, most specifically in China, Japan, and Southeast Asia. They prefer moist forest regions in mountains as high as 9900 ft/3000 m. Most interestingly, during the Miocene Period (about 12-30 million years ago) these newts could be also be found in Europe. The species shown here is *Tylototriton verrucosus*.

First described by Boulenger in 1886, *Rana camerani* is native to Russia, Turkey, and northerwestern Iran. It is generally agreed by most taxonomists that the *Rana* genus is far from being "solid." This species, for example, is thought by many to be in a subgenus, *Rana*, in what is known as the *Rana temporaria* group. ▶

The fire-bellied newts, genus *Cynops*, occasionally are seen in pet stores. In many ways these newts resemble those in the genus *Triturus*, which occur mainly in Europe. Species like this *Cynops ensicauda* do well in a largely aquatic setup with floating land bodies and a water temperature of about 65°F/18°C. ▶

◀ One of the most widespread of all frog and toad genera, *Rana* has about 140 extant species on the continent of Asia. Mostly medium-sized and very hardy, some make superb terrarium inmates and boast subtle but opulent colors. The specimen shown here, *Rana ornativentris*, is virtually never seen in the hobby of herpetology.

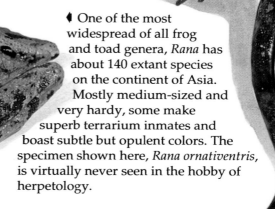

◀ Occurring in western China at elevations of up to 2500 m, *Rana phrynoides* in many ways resembles *Rana boulengeri*, also a native to western China. The latter, however, has black spines on its chest and abdomen. *R. phrynoides* was described in 1917.

Occurring only in China and Japan, the Oriental hellbenders, genus *Andrias*, have an interesting life history. They will hide in dark underwater cavities during the day and venture out during the night hours to hunt fish, worms, crayfish, and other amphibians. They grow to a respectable size— up to 1.8 m—and lay about 450 eggs per clutch. Seen here is *Andrias davidianus*. ▶

AFRICA & MADAGASCAR

Africa, the second largest continent in the world, is home to a vast array of herptofauna; unsurprising when one considers the entire continent falls almost completely within a climatic boundary known as the Tropical Zone. Beyond the southeastern tip of Africa, separated by the Mozambique Channel, is the island of Madagascar. It is the fourth largest island in the world, with a surface area of somewhere around 587,000 square km. It is generally believed Madagascar broke away from the African mainland about 140 million years ago.

◆ One of about 40 species of *Rana* that occur in Africa, *R. galamensis* haunts moist savannah regions. It is a fairly widespread animal and rarely grows over 3.2 in/8 cm. First described in 1841, there are currently two recognized subspecies.

◆ Frogs of the genus *Mantella* (which are at the moment being placed in their own family, Mantellidae) have recently made quite a splash in the herpetological hobby, particularly the species shown here, *M. cowani*. These tiny "micro-frogs" come in a variety of striking colors and patterns and bear more than a passing resemblance to the poison frogs, family Dendrobatidae. They are endemic to Madagascar.

A fairly large and often confused genus (taxonomically), members of *Boophis* are for the most part tree-dwellers that haunt high-elevation forest regions. They are active most often at night and have a pupil that varies from horizontally oblong to diamond-shaped, like the *B. pauliani* shown here. Occasionally, the irises will boast a bright coloration, the exact hue itself varying from specimen to specimen. *Boophis* is not often seen in captivity. ◄

Known in some circles as the "running frogs," members of the genus *Kassina* have earned that name from the fact that they seldom hop but instead actually appear to "run." Active mainly at night and almost exclusively terrestrial, they dig down deep into the earth during the dry seasons. They breed during the rainy season when floods saturate grasslands, bogs, and swamps. The species depicted is *Kassina senegalensis.* ▶

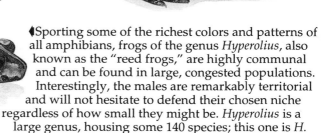

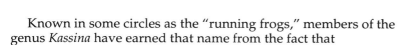

◄Sporting some of the richest colors and patterns of all amphibians, frogs of the genus *Hyperolius*, also known as the "reed frogs," are highly communal and can be found in large, congested populations. Interestingly, the males are remarkably territorial and will not hesitate to defend their chosen niche regardless of how small they might be. *Hyperolius* is a large genus, housing some 140 species; this one is *H. marmoratus.*

Only rarely seen in the hobby, African ghost frogs, genus *Heleophryne*, are usually active during the night, early morning, or dusk hours, and can be found both close to or very far from water. Not much has been learned about their reproductive biology, but it is known that their larva have a fairly long developmental period—up to two years. The species shown is *H. natalensis.* ▶

EUROPE

The continent of Europe is part of the Palearctic Region. The Palearctic contains quite a number of different climatic zones, and thus a large variety of habitats. This in turn, of course, lends opportunity for a broad assortment of fauna. In some areas European amphibians will experience sharply defined and often brutal winters, whereas in other zones such seasonal boundaries are much more mild. When keeping European amphibians in captivity it is vital that you know the animal's place of origin.

◄ Known as the Eurasian Treefrog, *Hyla arborea* occurs over much of the Palearctic Region. It tends to vary in color and pattern, but for the most part the species appears as seen here. A fairly reliable pet, it will thrive on a diet of small insects.

◄ Members of the genus *Discoglossus* bear more than a passing resemblance to those in *Rana*, the main differences being the round or heart-shaped pupil and the unobtrusive tympanum. Known as the "painted frogs," discoglossids frequent sunlit swamps and cool mountain streams, but, most interestingly, have also been known to haunt brackish water localities as well. The one shown here is *Discoglossus jeanae*.

▶ The Northern Crested Newt, *Triturus cristatus*, is still fairly common in Europe but declining to the point where it is now protected by law. It rarely grows over 6.4 in/16 cm and usually is a dark grayish black on the back, contrasted by a brightly colored belly, usually orange. Captive specimens require a large water area and a reliable supply of small insects but occasionally will take pieces of raw meat.

◀ One of the very few herptiles with a trinomial name repeating one word, *Bufo bufo bufo* (also known as the Eurasian Common Toad) is quite a widespread animal—its range stretches into Europe, North Africa, and Asia to Japan. There are a number of described subspecies, but most are basically an earthy brown color.

◀ Perhaps the most commercially successful European salamander, on a global basis, is the Fire Salamander, *Salamandra salamandra*. One of the more attractive and hardy of all the caudates, thousands of specimens are sold within the pet trade every year and many of them are captive-bred. They will survive on a simple insect diet and do not require extensive heating.

The ribbed newts, genus *Pleurodeles* (*P. waltl* is shown here), can be found in parts of North Africa, Ibera, and the Meditteranean Islands in warm, still water bodies where much vegetation is present. They are crepuscular and very bold, aggressive little creatures. ◀

▶ The fire-bellied toads, genus *Bombina*, are among the most often sold anurans in the world. There are somewhere around a half-dozen species, but only one or two are seen in the hobby. Most of them, like this *Bombina orientalis*, can survive on a diet of crickets sprinkled with a vitamin supplement.

WHAT'S IN A NAME?

The subject of etymology, particularly in regard to the names of animals, can be both interesting and enlightening. By definition, etymology is the study of both the structure and history of words. An interested and attentive student often can learn quite a lot about the animal he or she is studying just from their name. Taxonomy, which is the process of scientifically naming and defining living things, is a vital aspect of natural history in the sense that one should realize names are not simply applied without basis—most names have meaning. Since scientific names are usually molded from Latin (and Greek) derivatives, it will take some time for the layman to adjust to some of the strange inflections and pronunciations, but the results can be very rewarding.

It would not be illogical to assume that Jefferson's Salamander, *Ambystoma jeffersonianum*, was named after the United States's third President and author of the Declaration of Independence, Thomas Jefferson. The truth, however, is that the name was inspired by Jefferson College in Canonsburg, Pennsylvania, which in turned was named after the famous figure mentioned above.

Often a species name will reflect the locality where the original specimen was taken. The Yonahlossee Salamander, *Plethodon yonahlossee*, for example, is named for Yonahlossee Road, near Linville, North Carolina, where the type-specimen was found. ➤

WHAT'S IN A NAME?

The popular and breathtaking Dyeing Poison Frog, *Dendrobates tinctorius*, bases its species name on the Latin *tinct*, which means "dyed." The species name in particular is an adjectival variant meaning "of or belonging to dyeing." The name came from the story that Indians would remove a feather from a parrot, place the frog on the remaining spot, and then when a new feather grew in place it would be any one of a few bright colors—yellow, red, blue, or whatever. The frog had "dyed" the bird. ◆

Sometimes a species name will make sense in its own context, but cause confusion when applied to the animal that bears it. The Black-bellied Salamander, for example, is known as *Desmognathus quadrimaculatus*, the second word being the Latin for "four-spotted," which doesn't seem to fit the animal at all. While it is true that most specimens are lightly spotted laterally (on the sides), the reason they have been specifically denoted in a group of four is because apparently there were four spots on the original specimen.

Sometimes the basis for a species name seems unclear, and, unfortunately, the author of the original description will not leave us any clues to follow up on. In the case of the Western Red-backed Salamander, *Plethodon vehiculum*, for example, "vehiculum" means "a means of transport," but doesn't really serve to explain anything. ◆

◆ In some cases, even a casual observer can ascertain the reasoning behind a scientific name. This particular poison frog is known as *Epipedobates tricolor*, and the species name means "three-colored." From the general appearance of the animal, virtually anyone can figure out where the binomial moniker came from.

INDEX

Page numbers in **boldface** refer to illustrations.